C002750031 4

KW-551-486

EDINBURGH CITY LIBRARIES

Please return/renew this item by the last date shown.
To renew quote your borrower number.
Corstorphine 529 5506
R.L102

2 - OCT 2006
9 NOV 2006
18 JAN 2007
12 FEB 2007
06 MAR 2007
02 MAY 2007
16 AUG 2007
14 JAN 2008
25 MAR 2008
22 APR 2008
22 MAY 2008
11 NOV 2008
19 DEC 2008
26 JAN 2009
06 MAR 2009
28 MAR 2009
14 AUG 2009
22 SEP 2009
29 OCT 2009
10 NOV 2009
19 OCT 2010
04 NOV 2010
24 NOV 2010
18 DEC 2010

Edinburgh City Libraries Ce	
C0027500031 4	
Askews	16-Aug-2006
PB	£7.99

Barbie™ Numbers Book

1 one

2 two

3 three

LONDON, NEW YORK, MUNICH,
MELBOURNE AND DELHI

Designer Thelma-Jane Robb
Editor Amy Junor
Senior Editor Catherine Saunders
Publishing Manager Simon Beecroft
Brand Manager Lisa Lanzarini
Category Publisher Alex Allan
Production Rochelle Talary
DTP Designer Hanna Ländin

First published in Great Britain in 2006
by Dorling Kindersley Limited,
80 Strand, London WC2R 0RL

Published in Australia by
Dorling Kindersley Pty Ltd
250 Camberwell Road, Camberwell, Victoria 3124

A Penguin Company

06 07 08 09 10 10 9 8 7 6 5 4 3 2 1

BARBIE and associated trademarks and trade dress are owned by, and used under license from, Mattel, Inc.
Copyright © 2006 Mattel, Inc. All rights reserved.

Page design © 2006 Dorling Kindersley Limited

All rights reserved. No part of this publication may be reproduced, stored in a retrieval system, or transmitted in any form or by any means, electronic, mechanical, photocopying, recording, or otherwise, without the prior written permission of the copyright owner.

ISBN-13: 978-1-40531-366-7
ISBN-10: 1-4053-1366-8

Reproduced by Media Development and Printing, Ltd.
Printed and bound in China by Toppan Printing Co. Ltd.

Acknowledgements
Barbie® doll photography by the Mattel Photo Studio.

All other non-Barbie® images © Dorling Kindersley www.dkimages.com

Additional photography by Jon Bouchier, Paul Bricknell, Jane Burton, Gordon Clayton, Andy Crawford, Geoff Dann, Philip Dowell, Mike Dunning, Steve Gorton, Steve Gorton and Karl, Frank Greenaway, Marc Henrie, Dave King, Bill Ling, Stephen Oliver, Susanna Price, Tim Ridley, Jules Selmes, Steve Shott, James Stevenson, Harry Taylor, Matthew Ward, Barry Watts, Andrew Whittuck, Jerry Young.

The publisher would also like to thank the staff at Mattel, Inc., especially Vicki Jaeger, Monica Okazaki, and Judy Tsuno.

Discover more at
www.dk.com

Barbie™
Numbers Book

DK

How to use this book

Barbie™ Numbers Book is the perfect way to learn about numbers and basic maths. It features themes and images that children love and can relate to, such as birthday parties, baby animals and dressing up. First of all, Barbie leads your child through basic counting, starting from one to ten and going all the way up to one hundred! Next Barbie introduces simple maths problems, showing how to add, subtract, divide and multiply. Read this book aloud and watch your child's understanding of numbers grow. And most of all, have fun!

Contents

Learn to **count** from **one** to **ten**

1 one

4 four

7 seven

9 nine

2 two

3 three

5 five

6 six

8 eight

Say each number out loud as you count.

10 ten

Keep practising until you feel confident.

Learn to count at bedtime

1

wardrobe

4

blankets

7

toothbrushes

9

lamps

2

beds

3

nightdresses

5

dressing gowns

6

clocks

8

cushions

10

teddy bears

Count these bedtime objects.

How many clocks are there?

How many beds are there?

How many lamps are there?

Mix it up!

1

6

jacket

necklaces

jumpers

hats

t-shirts

bags

2 3 4 5

7 8 9 10

coats

skirts

dresses

shorts

Match them up!

The numbers from one to ten are in the correct order, but the groups of clothes are all mixed up.

Can you match the numbers to the groups of clothes?

How many baby animals?

8

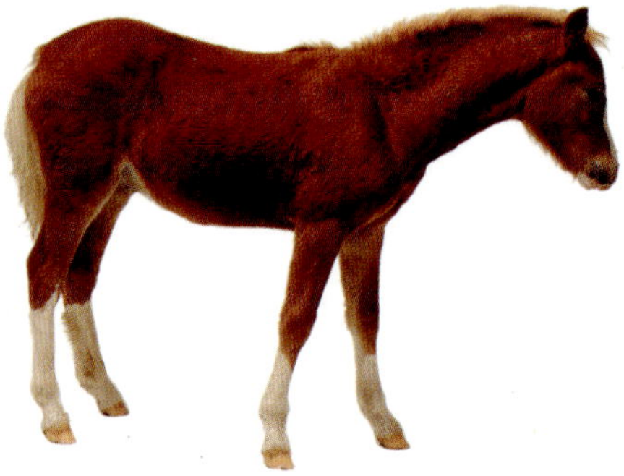

foal

hamsters

2

piglets

1

9

4

puppies

goats

7

chicks

5

3

rabbits

10

kittens

lambs

6

calves

Mix and match

Count the baby animals and find the number that matches.

How many kittens are there?

How many lambs are there?

Which number is missing?

1

1	2 tiaras	3	4 tiaras
2 dresses	?	4 dresses	5
4	5 jewels	6	7 jewels

2

castles

3

4

castles

?

5

6

tiaras

?

8

tiaras

6

dresses

?

?

9

jewels

Find the number!

Each sequence has a missing number.

What are the missing numbers?

Top tip Say each sequence out loud!

To make it harder, the last two sequences don't start at number one!

Now learn to **count** from **eleven** to **twenty**!

11 eleven

14 fourteen

17 seventeen

19 nineteen

12 twelve

13 thirteen

15 fifteen

16 sixteen

18 eighteen

20 twenty

Which number comes after eleven?

Which number comes before twenty?

Learn to **count** at a **birthday party**

11

birthday cakes

14

sandwiches

17

ice cream sundaes

19

lollipops

12

drinks

13

ice creams

15

sweets

16

cupcakes

18

biscuits

20

jellies

How many cupcakes are there?

How many biscuits are there?

Now you can **count** from **one** to **twenty**!

1
one

2
two

6
six

7
seven

8
eight

9
nine

11
eleven

12
twelve

13
thirteen

14
fourteen

16
sixteen

17
seventeen

18
eighteen

19
nineteen

3
three

4
four

5
five

10
ten

15
fifteen

20
twenty

Now it's your turn!

It's time to put together all the things you have learnt so far.

Count the numbers from one to twenty.

Which number comes after ten?

Which number comes before fifteen?

Which number comes after eight?

Pairs

2

shells

8

flippers

10

starfish

=

equals

14

fish

If there are fourteen fish, how many pairs of fish are there?

=

equals

1 pair of shells

=

equals

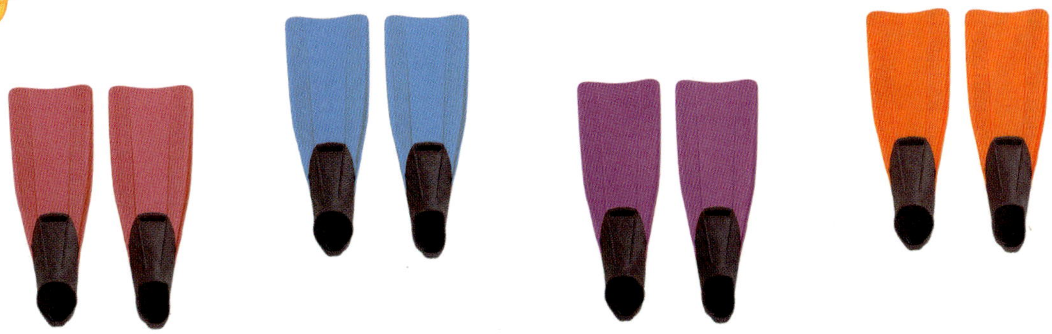

4 pairs of flippers

5 pairs of starfish

=

equals

?

pairs of fish

Pairs

Pairs are groups of two objects that look the same.

To find out how many pairs there are, put the objects that look the same into groups of two.

Odd and even numbers

1

6

drums

7

8

trumpets

11

12

tambourines

13

16

maracas

17

18

bells

2

pianos

3

4

guitars

5

9

10

violins

Even numbers

An even number of objects can be paired up. Each even number on this page is blue and has a group of pictures beside it.

14

musical notes

15

19

20

recorders

Odd numbers

When an odd number of objects are paired up, there is always one left over. All the odd numbers on this page are pink.

How many?

feather boas

dress-up box

jewellery boxes

rings

fairy wings

hats

lipsticks

1 2 3 4 5 6 7 8 9 10 11 12 13 14 15 16 17 18 19 20

bags

masks

Dress Up!

Barbie loves to dress up.

Count how many there are of each item.

Can any groups of items be paired up?

How many groups contain an odd number of items?

nail polish

wands

pairs of shoes

Learn to **count** in **tens**!

10
ten

40
forty

70
seventy

90
ninety

20
twenty

30
thirty

50
fifty

60
sixty

80
eighty

Now that you can count up to twenty, look how easy it is to count in tens to one hundred!

100
one hundred

Top tip Each of these numbers begins with one of the numbers from one to ten that you already know!

Adding

2 presents

4 balloons

plus

3 balloons

5 party bags

plus

4 party bags

6 party hats

plus

4 party hats

\+ plus

4 presents

= equals

6 presents

= equals

7 balloons

= equals

9 party bags

= equals

10 party hats

Now it's your turn!

Use what you have learnt to solve these problems

$4 + 2 = ?$

$2 + 8 = ?$

$9 + 1 = ?$

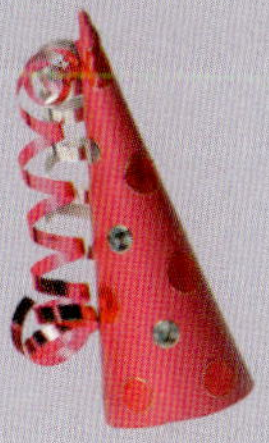

$3 + 3 = ?$

$4 + 5 = ?$

$6 + 3 = ?$

$1 + 7 = ?$

More adding

10 kites

5 flowers

+

plus

5 flowers

8 balls

+

plus

3 balls

7 leaves

+

plus

7 leaves

\+  = 

plus 1 kite equals 11 kites

\+  = 

plus 10 flowers equals 20 flowers

\+  = 

plus 4 balls equals 15 balls

\+  = 

plus 5 leaves equals 19 leaves

Subtracting

3 deck chairs

6 swim rings

minus

2 swim rings

10 sandcastles

minus

5 sandcastles

8 swimsuits

minus

6 swimsuits

− minus	 2 deck chairs	= equals	 1 deck chair
= equals	 4 swim rings		
= equals	 5 sandcastles		
= equals	 2 swimsuits		

Now try these!

Subtraction simply means to take away, or to minus.

If there are three deck chairs and you take two deck chairs away, you have one deck chair left.

This means :

$$3 - 2 = 1$$

$$6 - 3 = ?$$

$$8 - 5 = ?$$

$$4 - 3 = ?$$

$$3 - 1 = ?$$

More subtracting

14 scarves

20 umbrellas

12 snowmen

—

minus

3 snowmen

20 winter hats

—

minus

6 winter hats

—		=	
minus	2 scarves	equals	12 scarves
—		=	
minus	3 umbrellas	equals	17 umbrellas
—		=	
minus	5 snowmen	equals	4 snowmen
—		=	
minus	9 winter hats	equals	5 winter hats

Dividing or shared between

4 apples

÷

shared between

6 bananas

÷

shared between

2 people

6 cherries

÷

shared between

3 people

=

equals

9 oranges

÷

shared between

3 people

=

equals

2 people

equals

2 apples each

equals

3 bananas each

2 cherries each

3 oranges each

Simple sharing!

Dividing is another way of saying "shared between". If Barbie has lunch with Teresa and they share six bananas between two people, they would have three bananas each. That means

$$6 \div 2 = 3$$

More dividing

6 ribbons

9 tutus

8 leotards

÷

divided by

2

12 hair clips

÷

divided by

3

÷ divided by 2 = equals

3 ribbons

÷ divided by 3 = equals

3 tutus

= equals

4 leotards

= equals

4 hair clips

Try it yourself!

Work out the answers to these division sums.

$6 \div 3 = ?$

$8 \div 4 = ?$

$10 \div 2 = ?$

$16 \div 8 = ?$

$10 \div 5 = ?$

$18 \div 2 = ?$

$20 \div 10 = ?$

Counting in twos

2

8

14

18

4

6

10

12

16

20

Counting in twos is a great way to start learning your two times table!

To find the next number, just add two every time.

Learn the **two times table!**

2

two

2 two	x times	 2 plates
2 two	x times	 3 chairs
2 two	x times	 4 cups

x

times

1 sofa

=

equals

2 sofas

=

equals

4 plates

=

equals

?

=

equals

?

Multiplying

Multiplying is a way to add groups with the same number of objects.

2 x 3 means three groups of two objects each.

$2 + 2 + 2 = 6$

It doesn't matter which number is first.

$3 \times 2 = 6$

$2 \times 3 = 6$

Two times table

1 x 2 = 2	7 x 2 = 14
2 x 2 = 4	8 x 2 = 16
3 x 2 = 6	9 x 2 = 18
4 x 2 = 8	10 x 2 = 20
5 x 2 = 10	11 x 2 = 22
6 x 2 = 12	12 x 2 = 24

More multiplying

1

one

2

two

x

times

3

three

x

times

2 sweatbands

4

four

x

times

2 shuttlecocks

=

equals

x

times

1 ball

=

equals

1 ball

1 tennis racket

=

equals

2 tennis rackets

=

equals

6 sweatbands

8 shuttlecocks

More multiplying!

Can you solve these problems?

2 x 2 = ?

2 x 3 = ?

4 x 3 = ?

Times tables

Times tables are lists of all the ways numbers can be multiplied.

Try learning all the times tables in the back of this book!

Fun sums

Good job!

Now you've learnt how to count from one to twenty and how to add, subtract, multiply and divide! Here's some more practice sums.

+ add

— subtract

÷ divide

x multiply

$5 + 4 = ?$

$15 + 5 = ?$

$12 + 2 = ?$

$10 + 3 = ?$

$16 + 4 = ?$

$19 - 16 = ?$

$12 - 10 = ?$

$17 - 7 = ?$

$10 - 3 = ?$

$16 - 13 = ?$

$20 \div 5 = ?$

$12 \div 2 = ?$

$15 \div 3 = ?$

$20 \div 2 = ?$

$16 \div 4 = ?$

2 x 5 = ?

3 x 4 = ?

2 x 8 = ?

4 x 2 = ?

5 x 3 = ?

1 x table

1	x	1	=	1
2	x	1	=	2
3	x	1	=	3
4	x	1	=	4
5	x	1	=	5
6	x	1	=	6
7	x	1	=	7
8	x	1	=	8
9	x	1	=	9
10	x	1	=	10
11	x	1	=	11
12	x	1	=	12

2 x table

1	x	2	=	2
2	x	2	=	4
3	x	2	=	6
4	x	2	=	8
5	x	2	=	10
6	x	2	=	12
7	x	2	=	14
8	x	2	=	16
9	x	2	=	18
10	x	2	=	20
11	x	2	=	22
12	x	2	=	24

5 x table

1	x	5	=	5
2	x	5	=	10
3	x	5	=	15
4	x	5	=	20
5	x	5	=	25
6	x	5	=	30
7	x	5	=	35
8	x	5	=	40
9	x	5	=	45
10	x	5	=	50
11	x	5	=	55
12	x	5	=	60

6 x table

1	x	6	=	6
2	x	6	=	12
3	x	6	=	18
4	x	6	=	24
5	x	6	=	30
6	x	6	=	36
7	x	6	=	42
8	x	6	=	48
9	x	6	=	54
10	x	6	=	60
11	x	6	=	66
12	x	6	=	72

9 x table

1	x	9	=	9
2	x	9	=	18
3	x	9	=	27
4	x	9	=	36
5	x	9	=	45
6	x	9	=	54
7	x	9	=	63
8	x	9	=	72
9	x	9	=	81
10	x	9	=	90
11	x	9	=	99
12	x	9	=	108

10 x table

1	x	10	=	10
2	x	10	=	20
3	x	10	=	30
4	x	10	=	40
5	x	10	=	50
6	x	10	=	60
7	x	10	=	70
8	x	10	=	80
9	x	10	=	90
10	x	10	=	100
11	x	10	=	110
12	x	10	=	120